New Mags City Guide
Copenhagen

For years, I've traveled the world as a design and lifestyle expert. Every time I discover an inspiring place, I make a note of it. Over time, this list has grown to include many outstanding destinations. People often ask me for travel recommendations. Obviously, most people don't have the time to find the best spots, because it requires time, and time is a scarce resource for many. That's why we created this series of city guides. Not just any collection of guides, but the best, most beautiful, and most practical, presented as a real book. I believe the ideal city guide is tangible, something you can bring along on your journey, especially handy when your smartphone runs out of battery.

Special thanks to Jesper Svangaard from New Mags for his enthusiasm and publishing expertise, and to Mario Depicolzuane, our art director, whose studio's design brought this guide to life. I'm also deeply grateful to all the incredible locations featured and to everyone who helped bring this project to life.

We hope that you, as a reader, will embrace our city guide and find it valuable on your travels. After all, that's the true purpose of this book.

TABLE OF CONTENTS

Front Cover & Destination Photos by Tobias Glud

Copenhagen embodies the best of many cities. It captures Berlin's raw energy, Paris's refined elegance, London's effortless cool, and Amsterdam's inviting coziness. While it may lack a skyline of towering skyscrapers, Copenhagen makes up for it with its own striking silhouette of historic towers, often called the "City of Towers." You'll never run out of things to do here. It's the kind of place where FOMO isn't just a feeling—it's practically a chronic condition. Over the past few decades, Copenhagen has undergone a remarkable transformation,

evolving from a lesser-known city into an internationally acclaimed metropolis, celebrated for its design, gastronomy, and laidback lifestyle. Here, biking isn't merely a mode of transport; it's a way of life. Whether you're exploring on two wheels, on foot, or hopping onto the Metro, introduced in 2002, you'll feel the city's distinct rhythm. Despite its modest size, Copenhagen is a patchwork of diverse neighborhoods, each with its own unique character and charm. That's exactly why this guide will be your perfect companion as you set out to explore the city.

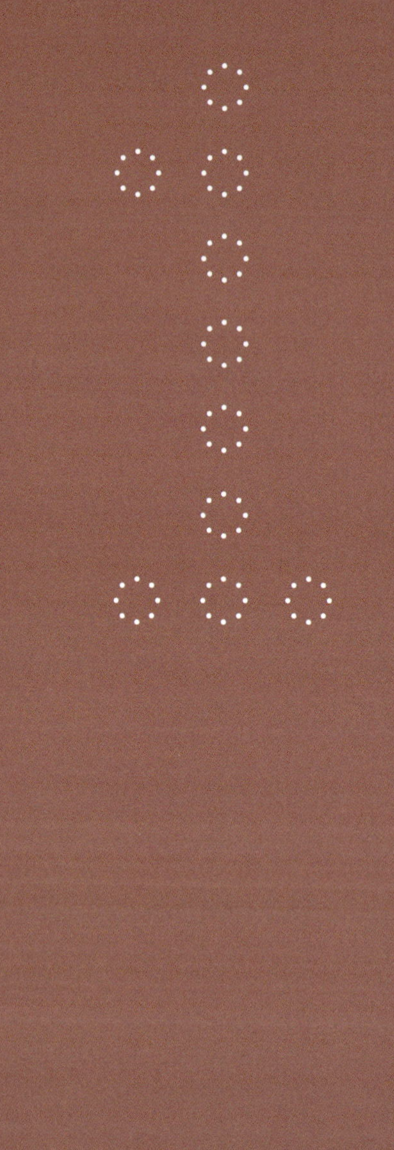

25hours Hotel Paper Island
Hotel Sanders
Coco Hotel
Villa Copenhagen
Hotel Bella Grande
Nobis Copenhagen
Hotel Ottilia
Kaj Hotel
The Central Hotel

Stay

25hours Hotel Paper Island

Papirøen 25
1436 Copenhagen

@25hourshotels_copenhagen
25hours-hotel.com
+45 7077 0701

The 25hours Hotel Paper Island is the second hotel in Copenhagen from the Hamburg-based hotel chain. The building is located on Christiansholm Island, also known as Paper Island, just a few steps from Nyhavn and the Inner City. The Paper Island has been transformed into a vibrant new neighborhood, featuring pioneering architecture by the award-winning Cobe architects. 25hours is known for its playful and eclectic style, and this hotel is no exception. Inside, the design solutions by Swedish firm Stylt Trampoli evokes the feeling of a Scandinavian holiday home on a small island. The result is a hotel with 128 rooms, and six with private outdoor areas and an Asian restaurant. The hotel also features a small shop reflecting the variety of items you might find in such a place, from fishing gear to shoes and food.

Enjoy the hotels eclectic, playful aesthetic and explore the newly established Paper Island.

NATURAL SOAP

Hotel Sanders

Tordenskjoldsgade 15
1055 Copenhagen

@hotelsanders
hotelsanders.com
+45 4640 0040

When you step into Hotel Sanders, it feels like entering a film or a theater piece from a bygone era, somewhere between Blixens African Farm and British colonial style. Founded by renowned ballet dancer Alexander Kølpin, and in collaboration with designers Lind + Almond, the hotel has created a concept unlike anything else in Copenhagen. Since its opening in 2017, the hotel has been the city's most fashionable, a status it still enjoys. The hotel features 53 luxurious rooms, each uniquely styled and designed. Various accommodations cater to the needs of every guest. The single rooms are inspired by the opulent train cabins of a bygone era, offering comfort and luxury within an intimate space while Sanders suites provide the utmost privacy with generous space, separate lounge areas, and open fireplaces. Don't miss the courtyard. This inner sanctuary is covered and during the colder months an open wood burning fireplace is the perfect place to hang out.

Hotel Sanders is beautifully choreographed as a modern interpretation of Karen Blixen's "Out of Africa" and classic colonial style.

COCO
COCO
HOTEL
CAFE
&
BAR
MON-FRI
SAT & SUN

Coco Hotel

Vesterbrogade 41
1620 Copenhagen

@cocohotel.dk
coco-hotel.com
+45 3321 2166

Located in the heart of the hip Vesterbro district, The Coco hotel is best described as a small Parisian-style hotel curated with a touch of Scandinavian minimalism. Each room is uniquely decorated with individual details that bring authentic personality and appearance to the spaces. Opened in the fall of 2019, the hotel offers 90 rooms. On the first floor, Café Coco, with direct access to the lush courtyard, is open to everyone throughout the day. The hotel is owned by the Danish restaurant group Cofoco, a food collaborative which operates 16 restaurants in Copenhagen and two hotels, including Coco and the newest addition, Bella Grande (p. 33). Like all Cofoco restaurants, Coco was designed with the belief that great hospitality can be both affordable and sustainable. From morning to night, everything revolves around the sun, whether it's streaming through the dormer windows of each room or powering the lights at night with electricity generated by Cofoco's own solar field.

26

Stay at this award-winning hotel, where Parisian style meets Nordic minimalism.

UBAC
ALOUIN
pol bury
RIOPELLE
ficelles et autres jeux

Villa Copenhagen

Tietgensgade 35-39
1577 Copenhagen

@villacph
villacopenhagen.com
+45 7873 0000

Inside the former Central Post Office building in Copenhagen, a new hotel concept unfolded in the spring of 2020. The impressive Neo-Baroque building next to the Tivoli Gardens and Copenhagen Central Station was carefully restored to appear exactly as it did for its inauguration in 1912 when the Danish postal service moved their headquarters to the address. Today, Villa Copenhagen is an outstanding hotel that has found the perfect sweet spot of laid-back luxury.

All 390 rooms are designed with careful attention to the original architecture and uncompromising craftsmanship. The hotel also features an impressive atrium, a modern bar, a restaurant, and even a rooftop pool—a rarity among Copenhagen hotels and a popular spot even for locals who check in just to hang out by the pool. Villa Copenhagen is part of the growing collection of Nordic Hotels & Resorts, owned by Norwegian billionaire Petter Stordalen.

The pool alone is reason enough to choose Villa Copenhagen, but exploring the old post office building completes the experience.

Hotel Bella Grande

Vester Voldgade 23
1552 Copenhagen

@hotelbellagrande
hotelbellagrande.com
+45 7060 1021

Hotel Bella Grande made a remarkable debut in 2024 as the sister property to the prestigious Coco Hotel (p. 25). Situated just steps away from City Hall square in a historic building from 1899, the hotel seamlessly blends the essence of authentic Copenhagen with a touch of Italian charm and nostalgia. From the moment you step into the reception, you're carried away to another era. Instead of modern key cards, guests are handed traditional keys with tassels, and the lobby, the heart of the hotel, exudes the warm ambiance of Italy's classic coastal hotels. For those craving more Italian nostalgia, a visit to the hotel's restaurant Donna is a must, offering iconic dishes from the Italian cuisine. Hotel Bella Grande is not only a grand destination but also a charming and intimate retreat in the vibrant heart of Copenhagen.

Bella Grande offers a perfect mix of Italian charm and authentic Copenhagen vibe, the best of both worlds.

Nobis Copenhagen

Niels Brocks Gade 1
1574 Copenhagen

@nobishotelcopenhagen
nobishotel.dk
+45 7874 1410

There is something truly grand and magnificent about Nobis Copenhagen, and it's more than just its five-star rating. Perhaps it's the historic 1903 building, one of Copenhagen's first concrete structures, that once housed the Royal Danish Conservatory of Music. Or maybe it's the stunning location, nestled near the Ny Carlsberg Glyptotek Museum and Tivoli Gardens. The interiors, designed by renowned Swedish architects Gert Wingårdh and Wingårdhs, blending original elegance with contemporary materials like marble, stone, wood, and glass. It could be the seamless fusion of these remarkable features that makes this 80-room hotel stand out as a destination of unmatched charm and modernist sophistication.

Hotel Ottilia

Bryggernes Plads 7
1799 Copenhagen

@brochnerhotels
brochner-hotels.dk
+45 3338 7030

Hotel Ottilia is a cool industrial boutique hotel with 155 rooms, located in the historic Carlsberg brewery buildings now part of Copenhagen's Carlsberg City District. This vibrant area blends historic charm with urban vibe featuring trendy retailers, cafés, artisan bakeries and restaurants. Named in honor of Ottilia Marie Jacobsen, wife of Carlsberg's prominent brewer Carl Jacobsen, the hotel incorporates thistle motifs, reflecting her love for the flower.

The architecture and interior design solutions preserve the industrial character of the listed buildings, showcasing original concrete walls, solid pillars, and exposed beams. The hotel is housed in two original buildings that were once used for grain and beer storage. One of these buildings stands out with its façade decorated with 64 golden shields, reminiscent of the bottoms of beer bottles. In 2020, AIRE Ancient Baths opened at Hotel Ottilia, offering guests and locals a luxurious retreat with thermal baths, massages, and exceptional wellness experiences.

Kaj Hotel

Danneskiold-Samsøes Allé 57
1434 Copenhagen

@kajhotel
kajhotel.dk
+45 6168 3336

Kaj is neither a hotel nor a houseboat in the traditional sense. If you're looking for a different hotel experience, check into this tiny hotel located on the water near Refshaleøen. It is tucked away in Holmen, a quiet part of the beautiful harbor, offering a direct view of inner city just across the water and just a stone's throw from the vibrant Refshaleøen. So Kaj Hotel blends the perfect location with a truly unique living experience.

In addition to being a traditional Danish name, "Kaj" also means "quay" or "wharf," symbolically keeping the floating hotel grounded. Kaj Hotel was built following the same principles as most Danish houseboats: primarily from recycled and surplus materials. This approach makes the construction and maintenance process ever evolving, where the discovery of, for example, an old door or window or even the smallest detail, can influence design choices and decisions along the way.

If you're looking for a different hotel experience, check into this tiny hotel located on the water near Refshaleøen.

HOTEL
CENTRAL
& CAFÉ

The Central Hotel and Café

Tullinsgade 1
1618 Copenhagen

@centralhotelogcafee
centralhotelogcafe.dk
+45 3321 0095

The Central Hotel, despite having only one double room, is already a design landmark in Copenhagen. Located on top of The Central Café in the Vesterbro neighbourhood and just steps away from the city's coziest street, Værnedamsvej, it offers a one-of-a-kind experience.

The room of Central Hotel has a unique interior design with beautiful, handcrafted details that will make even the pickiest boutique hotel aficionado feel right at home. The charming side building, over 100 years old, originally housed a shoemaker's workshop with a small apartment above it. In 2011, the owners of the popular Granola café purchased the property and opened a café on the ground floor. As a guest, you'll enjoy a delicious breakfast from Granola, included with your stay.

Andersen & Maillard
Atelier September
Juno Bakery
Amator
Studio x Kitchen
Flere Fugle
Bottega Barlie
Restaurant Schønnemann
Graziano
La Banchina
Åben
Brasserie Post
Cafe Sommersko
Piola Pastificio
Restaurant Væksthuset
Bar Amore
Lille Blå
Bar Vitrine
Bird
Pompette

Taste

Andersen & Maillard

Antwerpengade 10
2150 Nordhavn

@andersenmaillard
andersenmaillard.dk
+45 33322322

Andersen & Maillard has gained cult status among locals for its innovative take on Danish baking and coffee roasting. Led by head baker Asger Hansen, the bakery offers modern twists on classic pastries. More than just a bakery, Andersen & Maillard is a go-to spot for coffee lovers, thanks to its in-house roastery, which attracts coffee enthusiasts from all over. With additional locations in Nørrebro and the Inner city district, the bakery has cemented its reputation as a staple in Copenhagen's food scene.

The interior design is a blend of Japanese and Scandinavian influences, creating a warm yet industrial feel. Soft textures, dark wooden furniture, and tactile details like a travertine countertop and a hand-carved Carrara marble sink enhance the inviting atmosphere, making Andersen & Maillard a true haven for those who appreciate craftsmanship, from the pastries to the coffee to the space itself.

Andersen & Maillard is the perfect pit stop for a well-brewed coffee and a freshly baked roll during your urban development tour of Nordhavn.

Atelier September

Kronprinsessegade 62
1306 Copenhagen

@atelierseptember
cafeatelierseptember.dk

Atelier September, founded in 2013 by chef Frederik Bille Brahe, was born from a vision of creating honest, everyday food crafted from beautiful, quality ingredients. Originally located on Gothersgade, the hyped café has since moved to Kronprinsessegade in central Copenhagen, with additional locations in Nordhavn and Hellerup.

Built on collaboration and the connection between kitchen, staff, and guests, Atelier September has gained a reputation for its signature dishes such the famous avo on rye. Operating during the day, Atelier September offers breakfast, lunch, speciality coffee, freshly pressed juices, tea, wine, and pastries across all its locations.

In 2023, in collaboration with Apartamento, Frederik published *Atelier September: A Place for Daytime Cooking*, a book that captures the café's first decade, sharing its celebrated recipes and delving into Frederik's philosophy on food and life.

PROLOG

Juno Bakery

Århusgade 48
2100 Copenhagen

@juno_the_bakery

Since opening in 2017, Juno the Bakery has seen lines stretching down Århusgade, with eager customers waiting to savour its iconic pastries. Founded by Emil Glaser, a former Noma chef, Juno quickly became a beloved spot in Østerbro. Its cinnamon buns, in particular, have gained massive popularity, and yes, they might just be the best in the world.

Today, Juno is a destination in its own right, attracting visitors from across the globe to its small bakery shop. But Juno is more than just a pastry haven. The bakery also excels in sourdough bread, made from organic grains, and its pistachio croissants, which have become local favourites. What truly sets Juno apart, however, is the meticulous craftsmanship behind every product, reflecting Glaser's unwavering commitment to quality and precision.

Juno the Bakery in Copenhagen is the most delicious bakery that more than lives up to its hype. Craving a cinnamon bun? Nothing beats Juno.

AMATOR
CURATED BY
MATI PICHCI
DESIGNED BY
WIERCINSKI-STUDIO

Amator

Nordre Frihavnsgade 7
2100 Copenhagen

@amatorcph

The intention behind Amator was to create a space that feels like home. With an open kitchen and a communal table, the concept is inspired by founder and chef Mati Pichci's social gatherings, as well as the apartment of his close friend, Adam Wiercinski, who also designed the interior and furniture.

Amator derives from the Latin word for "lover" or "devotee". When Mati moved to Copenhagen in 2019 for a three-month stage at Noma, he feared his lack of formal training would label him as an amateur. Now, he fully embraces his intuitive cooking style, using food to foster connections and build meaningful relationships. Amator has thus evolved into a "home dining place," with the mantra "join our table." Mati's signature dish, a classic omelette, remains the centerpiece of the menu. Open only during the day, Amator leans more towards a café than a restaurant, but its stylish decor and Mati's renowned omelette are reason enough to visit.

You'll love this little gem in Østerbro. Just look for the yellow sign and treat yourself to omelettes, a zen vibe, and great music.

JOIN OUR TA

Studio x Kitchen

Dronningens Tværgade 52
1302 Copenhagen

@studioxkitchen

Studio x Kitchen is among the trendiest cafés in the central Copenhagen, not far from Frederiksstaden, where similar übercool locations such as Atelier September, Frama, and Botega Barlie spread their distinct cool vibe to the district.

Immersed in this ultra-hip and lively environment, Studio x Kitchen draws in both fashionable locals and international influencers, to capture that perfect Instagram moment. The aesthetic is quite minimalist, cool, and distinctly Nordic. Food is served on simple ceramics plates, accompanied by light wooden furniture and soothing wall colors that create a calm, inviting space where you'll naturally want to linger. Breakfast and coffee are served in the morning, with light lunch options and indulgent pastries for those with a sweet tooth available throughout the day.

Head over to Studio x Kitchen for a cool spot to people-watch while enjoying a treat of delicious coffee, homebaked cake or a healthy, green lunch.

Flere Fugle

Rentemestervej 57
2400 Copenhagen

@flerefugle
flerefugle.dk
+45 9383 7573

Hidden in a converted garage on Rentemestervej, Flere Fugle, Danish for "more birds", is the beating heart of Nordvest's food scene. It's a bakery, pizza spot, and natural wine bar all in one. The space, now part of the city's Demokratigaragen project, feels like a cozy community hub where locals gather to enjoy fresh pastries, bistro-style dishes, and expertly brewed coffee from La Cabra.

The menu changes daily, but the standout is always their exceptional bread, made with ingredients sourced from local farms and mills. Whether you're grabbing a quick bite or lingering over a glass of natural wine, the vibe is laid-back and quintessentially Nordvest.

Although Flere Fugle is tucked away, the bakery has become quite a cult favourite, often drawing a long queue. With both indoor and outdoor seating, it's the perfect spot to soak in the authentic neighborhood atmosphere. And yes, their Instagram will definitely have you craving a visit.

The only spot in Nordvest to make it into this guide, and for good reason. This is one of the best bakeries in the city, making it well worth exploring the district.

SO
KI
SO
KI

Bottega Barlie

Fredericiagade 78
1310 Copenhagen

@bottegabarlie
barlie.dk
+45 2057 6750

Bottega Barlie is a local cafe, bistro, and wine bar situated on the corner of Fredericiagade in the Nyboder neighborhood in the heart of Copenhagen. Founded by two childhood friends, their vision was simple: create a welcoming space for locals to enjoy breakfast, lunch, and dinner throughout the week. At the heart of Bottega Barlie's kitchen is a dedication to vegetables and seafood, with a focus on local, seasonal ingredients. The menu evolves with the seasons, offering fresh and ever-changing dishes, while a few beloved staples remain year-round. Quality, consistency, and comfort define the dining experience here, making it a beloved spot for those who live and work nearby.

Building on the success of Bottega Barlie, the duo has expanded their vision with the opening of Bottega Estadio in Østerbro. While each location has its own personality, the philosophy remains the same: a laid-back, unpretentious atmosphere rooted in the local vibe, where you can always count on great food, a warm welcome, and a sense of community.

Bottega Barlie draws in fashionable Copenhageners with its perfect blend of wine bar, café, and tapas restaurant.

Bottega Barlie

Restaurant Schønnemann

Hauser Pl. 16
1127 Copenhagen

@restaurantschonnemann
restaurantschonnemann.dk
+45 3312 0785

Restaurant Schønnemann is more than just a restaurant; it's a slice of Danish culinary history, serving Copenhagen since 1877. Stepping inside feels like a journey back in time, with its dark wood paneling, green walls, and crisp white tablecloths setting the stage for a traditional Danish lunch. Smørrebrød, the famous open-faced sandwich, is the star of the show, and Schønnemann offers a staggering 110 variations, with 21 dedicated to herring alone. Pair your meal with one of their 140 brands of ice-cold schnapps, a quintessential Danish tradition.

People flock to this beloved spot for its hearty flavors and impeccable presentation. It's even said that Noma's René Redzepi invites guests here to experience the Danish tradition of rye bread with toppings. As it's a lunch-only destination, make it your main meal of the day. Be sure to book in advance, it's impossible to drop in without a reservation.

BOTTEGA

Graziano

Møllegade 12
2200 Copenhagen

@graziano_cph
graziano.dk
booking@graziano.dk

The Italian cuisine has made a strong impact on Copenhagen, but the new restaurant duo, Kaave Pour, formerly of Space10, and chef Jonathan B. Sørensen, are doing things differently with Graziano, a trattoria-inspired restaurant in the heart of Nørrebro.

Their concept is simple: a return to the roots, focusing on the raw elegance and simplicity of Tuscan food traditions. The menu features classic dishes like "Spaghetti al Pomodoro" (an homage to Jonathan's Italian grandfather), made with San Marzano tomatoes, alongside Bistecca alla Fiorentina and Tagliatelle al Ragù Bolognese, simply accompanied by the note: "No explanation needed."

This philosophy extends beyond the food to the restaurant's design. With Jonathan's Italian heritage and Kaave's background in design from Space10, the space draws inspiration from Italian Art Deco villas and Milanese palazzos, featuring hand-picked and recycled elements from local Italian suppliers, including iconic Aldo Jacober Trieste chairs and red terracotta tiles.

Truly Tuscan. Truly authentic. Truly delicious. Close your eyes, enjoy the food, and you'll find yourself dreaming of a Tuscan summer.

Trionfa Ferrari

La Banchina

Refshalevej 141
1432 Copenhagen

@labanchinacph
labanchina.dk
+45 31266561

La Banchina is a unique spot in Copenhagen. This cozy restaurant and wine bar with just 14 seats, is housed in a small wooden shed that once served as a waiting room for harbour workers. La Banchina is open every day serving breakfast and a daily selection of farm-to-table dishes. Expect no meat, only fish, along with great coffee, baked goods, snacks, and low-intervention wines. The menu is planned on the day and written on the windows. No reservations are needed, simply show up, find a spot in or around the charming blue house, and enjoy. From the pier next to the restaurant there is access to a small area which can be used for swimming and bathing year-round. You can even book a sauna session through the website.

After a refreshing dip in the cold harbour baths, treat yourself to delicious wine and food at Banchina. You've earned it.

LA BANCHINA
WELCOME TO THE VOLUNTEERING
GREENKAYAK LOCATION
ON YOUR ARRIVAL
1.
2.
3.
4.
LA BANCHINA
OPEN!
WINE
from 8OOAM
COFFEE
DELI GOODIES
BREAKFAST & DINNER
LUNCH

Åben

Slagtehusgade 15
1715 Copenhagen

@aabenbryg
aabenbryg.dk
+45 4068 6000

Located in the Meetpacking district, ÅBEN Brewery, Tank Bar & Restaurant serves freshly tapped beers and inspirational food. The building is a former slaughterhouse that has been transformed into a bar, restaurant and brewery designed by Pihlmann architects. All beers are brewed in the same building right behind the bar and restaurant. When the beer is finished, it flows directly to one of the 14 tanks hanging from the roof and into your glass. As a guest, you eat and drink in between the large brewing tanks while having full visibility of the open kitchen.

brasserie

Brasserie Post

Øster Allé 1
2200 Copenhagen

@brasseriepost
meyers.dk/restauranter/post
+45 28353034

Brasserie Post is located in the historic old post office building at "The Triangle" in Østerbro. Dating back to 1922, this iconic structure once housed postal operations but has since undergone a complete renovation. Opening its doors in 2023, Brasserie Post aims to be a stylish yet relaxed destination in a uniquely historic setting.

The chef, Dave Harrison, grew up and trained in Texas, later spending several years at the neo-bistro Au Passage in Paris. As a result, the menu features brasserie classics alongside modern interpretations of French countryside dishes.

During cold winter evenings, guests can enjoy the warmth of the bar and fireplace, while in summer, the Orangerie and courtyard provide a delightful outdoor experience. The bespoke interior design combines dark oak wood, vintage lamps, and intricate textiles, creating a space that honours the building's heritage and aesthetic.

Step into a neoclassical setting that could just as easily be in New York. However, the food is French, and the location is unmistakably Danish.

Cafe Sommersko

Palægade 6
1261 Copenhagen

@sommersko24
cafesommersko.dk
+45 7070 2329

If you belong to Generation X and spent your youth in Copenhagen in the '80s and '90s, you'll remember Café Sommersko on Kronprinsensgade. Your first cappuccino is like your first kiss, you never forget the feeling or the place. That's exactly what Café Sommersko was for many. It was the first of its kind in Denmark, heavily inspired by the café culture of Paris.

The original Café Sommersko closed in 2017 after a few turbulent years, but now it's reopening. Although it's moved to a new location in Palægade and won't physically resemble the original, the essence remains. The concept and menu have been refreshed to appeal to newer generations, but the soul of Sommersko lives on.

Leading the revival is restaurateur Nils Petter Bro, whose father and uncle originally opened Café Sommersko back in 1976.

Piola Pastificio

Thorvaldsensvej 2C
1871 Frederiksberg

@piola_pastificio
piola.dk
+45 6147 3462

Piola Pastificio is a small, family-run restaurant in Frederiksberg, owned and operated by the couple Antonio Errico and Johanne Ramskov. In Piemonte, a Piola is a place where you enjoy traditional food. Pastificio translates to "pasta factory," and that's exactly what Piola is: an authentic Italian restaurant where all the pasta is made fresh by hand every day.

Piola has 20 seats indoors, and the same number outdoors when the sun is shining. Antonio, born and raised in Puglia, is the head chef. The menu offers both a fixed selection and à la carte options. The focus is on traditional Italian dishes, using seasonal ingredients sourced from trusted local producers or imported directly from Italy.

Restaurant Væksthuset

Ekvipagemestervej 18
1438 Copenhagen

@vaeksthuset_operaparken
norrlyst.dk
+45 6110 1583

Restaurant Væksthuset boasts a truly unique location, nestled in the heart of the new Opera Park, with the Opera House on one side and Papirøen on the other. Opened in October 2023 to coincide with the park's inauguration, the restaurant was designed to blend seamlessly into the beautiful surroundings.

It's the perfect spot for a pre-show meal before heading to the Opera House, with a specially crafted opera menu that sets the tone for a memorable evening. If you're not into Opera and just want to enjoy the atmosphere of Væksthuset, you're welcome to do that too. On weekends, they serve classic breakfast dishes, traditional Danish smørrebrød for lunch, and a selection of Nordic-inspired dishes for dinner.

Stop by Restaurant Væksthuset on weekends and enjoy a delicious lunch surrounded by greenery in the impressive Operapark.

Bar Amore

Gl. Kongevej 74D
1850 Frederiksberg

@bar___amore
bar-amore.dk
+45 5377 6120

There is an Italian trend in the Copenhagen restaurant scene, but only a few locations really stand out. One of them is Bar Amore. Founder Philip Skovgaard grew up in Montalcino, Tuscany, so he knows his way around the Italian cuisine. For the past 10 years, he has been managing restaurants in Copenhagen with his wife, Lea Parkings Benjaminsen. First, they opened the wine and dining place Bevi Bevi, then the super popular restaurant Mangia, followed by Bar la Una, and most recently, the Tuscan-inspired Circolo, which is located side by side with Bar Amore in Frederiksberg.

Bar Amore is the couple's attempt to create a restaurant that lies somewhere between a wine bar and a restaurant, with an undogmatic approach to Italian cooking. It is a place where you can come in, drink a bottle of wine, and order as few or as many dishes as you like. Unlike the other restaurants that focus on a specific Italian region, Bar Amore serves dishes from all over Italy.

Don't let the hype distract you. Bar Amore may draw the cool crowd, but at its heart, it's pure, honest love for Italy and its cuisine.

TNT
matassa
little

Lille Blå

Esplanaden 3
1263 Copenhagen

@lilleblaavinbar
osterreich.dk
+45 3332 3911

Lille Blå (Little Blue) is a striking ultramarine wine bar located in a former paint store on the edge of the Inner city. Its focus is on natural wines, as well as traditional organic and biodynamic selections, mainly from Austria, with a few detours to Italy, France and Eastern Europe. The wine list is curated by the neighbouring wine importer and shop Österreich Vin, founded by Rind Nellemann and Christian Nedergaard, who also run Lille Blå and the renowned Copenhagen wine bar, Ved Stranden 10.

The bar features a Nordic minimalist design, with wooden interiors that create a blend of art gallery ambiance and wine bar charm. The atmosphere is friendly and informal, there is even flower on the tables, making it a welcoming spot for both locals and visitors. On sunny days head for the terrasse cause it's most likely buzzing with life. The bar is located right by the beautiful Kastellet. Just look for a white flag with a blue circle. The little blue dot marks the spot.

bar vitrine
TUE-SAT 11-23

Bar Vitrine

Møntergade 5
1116 Copenhagen

@bar_vitrine
barvitrine.dk

Bar Vitrine is an intimate 16-seat contemporary wine bar and eatery in the heart of Copenhagen. It's a creative collaboration between restaurateur Riccardo Marcon, chef Dhriti Arora, and Frama founder Niels Strøyer Christophersen, built on a shared passion for honest food, wine, and genuine conversation. The space features panoramic street-facing windows with steel frames and a warm, minimalist interior designed by Frama. A large birch communal table anchors the space, alongside cozy window seating offering views of Copenhagen's timeless architecture.

Bar Vitrine serves lunch, dinner, or simply a glass of wine with small plates. The wine list reflects Riccardo Marcon's focus on native grape varieties, terroir-driven wines, and sustainable winemaking, with a thoughtful selection available by the glass or bottle.

The hype around Bar Vitrine is well-deserved. Great natural wines, delicious small plates, impeccable decor, and a prime location on the city's hottest street.

Bird

Gl. Kongevej 102
1850 Frederiksberg

@bird.cph
birdcph.dk

Bird is a small neighborhood bar that emphasizes vinyl records, acoustics, and modern cocktails. It aims to blend exceptional drinking experiences with memorable musical moments through its bottled cocktail program and a deep passion for vinyl.

In its daily operations, Bird prioritizes the acoustic experience with a custom-designed sound system tailored for both cocktail lovers and audiophiles. Since opening in 2020, the bar has offered exclusively batched and bottled cocktails, with a menu of around 20 options, including both alcoholic and non-alcoholic choices.

With seating for over 45 guests, Bird focuses on minimizing preparation during service hours to maintain an acoustic-friendly environment, adhering to audiophile principles. The bar operates without using citrus ingredients, instead achieving balance through compound ingredients. Bird sells directly to private customers through its bottle shop and online store.

The only Danish cocktail bar to earn a spot on the prestigious list of the world's top 100 bars. Visit, and you'll see why it's well-deserved.

POMPETTE

Pompette

Møllegade 3
2200 Copenhagen

@pompettecph
etteetteette.dk

Pompette, meaning "tipsy" in French, is the ideal spot to enjoy a glass, or more, from a small but carefully curated selection of natural wines. Located in a cozy basement in the trendy Nørrebro neighbourhood, Pompette offers a friendly atmosphere and excellent wines, mostly natural, at very reasonable prices.

After years spent in France as a sommelier and briefly as a winemaker, and with a lifetime in the wine industry, owners Jesper Emil Norrie og Martin Ho opened Pompette in 2018 with a simple mission: make great wine accessible to everyone. A concept that truly appeals to the locals of Nørrebro. You can choose to enjoy the wine at Pompette or even take home, as the bar also doubles as a wine shop. If you get a little hungry, Pompette also offers a simple menu of charcuterie, cheeses, and small cold dishes, including their delightful burrata.

Pompette equals natural wine, hip Nørrebro crowd and affordable prices. Get a table outside on a sunny day.

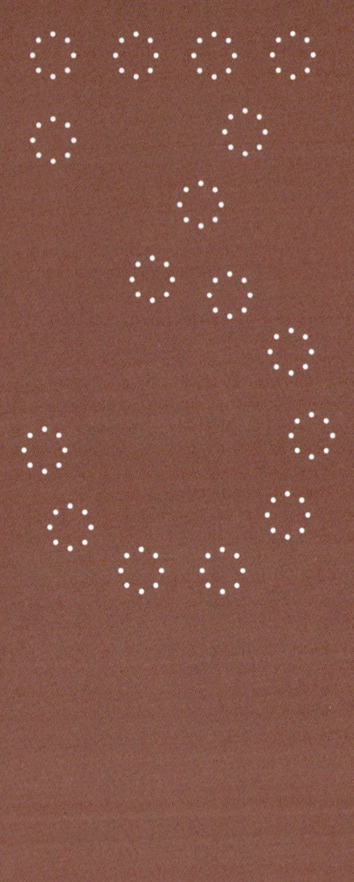

Trine Tuxen Jewelry
Frama
Helle Mardahl Studio
Another Aspect
Naked Copenhagen
Rue Verte
New Mags
Studio Oliver Gustav
Jerome Vintage
Edition Copenhagen
Nuvole Design
Tableau

Shop

Trine Tuxen Jewelry and Lifestyle Store

Elmegade 5
2200 Copenhagen

@trinetuxenjewelry
trinetuxenjewelry.com
+45 9393 5468

In December 2022, Trine Tuxen opened her newest venture, a jewelry and lifestyle store nestled in the vibrant neighborhood of Nørrebro, just steps from her own home. The space is a true reflection of Trine Tuxen's passions, showcasing not only her renowned jewelry but also an exciting new array of ceramics, a material she has recently embraced to further express her artistic vision. The store also features carefully selected fragrances and aromas, adding depth to the sensory experience. The new store was designed by Studio0405, who also originally designed and crafted the first store at Gl. Kongevej in Frederiksberg. In many ways, the store in Elmegade is a fine reinterpretation of the old, more nostalgic space in Frederiksberg.

Visiting the Elmegade store offers a comprehensive insight into the universe of Trine Tuxen, where every item tells a unique story.

With her new store in Nørrebro, jewelry designer Trine Tuxen has crafted a holistic lifestyle concept that extends the essence of her jewelry.

Frama

Fredericiagade 57
1310 Copenhagen

@framacph
framacph.com
+45 3140 6030

Nestled in the historic St. Pauls Apotek, Frama Studio Store in Copenhagen offers a serene blend of past and present, where 19th century charm meets contemporary design. This multi-disciplinary brand, founded by Niels Strøyer Christophersen, features a curated selection of furniture, lighting, and lifestyle products that emphasize clean lines, natural materials, and meticulous craftsmanship. Frama's space, adorned with original oak pharmaceutical cabinets and ornately painted ceilings, extends its philosophy to a unique scent collection designed to evoke calm and nostalgia.

The studio not only showcases design but also acts as a vibrant creative hub. With its adjoining eatery, Apotek 57, visitors can enjoy seasonal dishes amid an ambiance of thoughtful design and historical architecture. Frama is more than a store; it's a destination that offers a holistic experience, inviting guests to explore, dine, and connect with the essence of new Scandinavian aesthetics.

The unique Frama universe is a must-visit for those who appreciate aesthetics and good style.

Helle Mardahl Studio

Bredgade 17
1260 Copenhagen

@hellemardahl
hellemardahl.com
+45 3160 2502

Helle Mardahl Studio's new flagship store is located in a celebrated building in the heart of Copenhagen. Once home to a prestigious royal jeweller, the space has been thoughtfully restored and transformed, seamlessly blending historical architecture with her colourful, signature creations. The store embodies the essence of Helle Mardahl's dreamy universe of glossy glass design, crafting a conceptual candyland of magic, dreams, and indulgence.

Colour, a defining element of her brand, has been carefully applied to harmonise with the architectural setting. The palette, soft nude tones, delicate pinks, and creamy whites, creates an airy atmosphere that enhances the vibrancy of the glasswork. The space remains light, allowing the glass to take centre stage, with each piece given room to breathe and truly be seen.

Experience the magic of Helle Mardahl's world, a captivating blend of glass and pastel hues that promises to leave you spellbound.

Neighbourhoods

Indre By
Refshaleøen
Vesterbro
Nordhavn
Christianshavn
Østerbro
Nørrebro
Frederiksberg

Copenhagen

FOOD FOOD FOOD

PAPIRØEN
papiroen.dk

A cityscape is defined by the sum of its neighbourhoods. They are the heartbeat of a city, infusing life and diversity into its very soul. Some are artsy and vibrant, others are more serene and exclusive. Each neighbourhood has its own unique character, and we allhave our favourite areas that we feel connected to. In this section, we break down the city and introduce you to the coolest neighbourhoods. All the locations in the book, along with a few bonus spots, are marked on detailed neighbourhood maps, making it easy for you to discover your favourite district.

E

3
6
8
12
4
5
7
9
19
15
10
11
14
13
1
18
16
17
2

Indre By (Inner City)

1	Hotel Sanders (p. 21)	8	Lille Blå Vinbar (p. 103)	15	Helle Mardahl Studio (p. 127)
2	Nobis Copenhagen (p. 37)	9	New Mags Bookstore (p. 141)	16	Garden of the Royal Library (p. 193)
3	Atelier September (p. 53)	10	Another Aspect (p. 131)	17	Ny Carlsberg Glyptotek (p. 177)
4	Studio x Kitchen (p. 63)	11	Naked Cph (p. 137)	18	Thorvaldsens Museum (p. 163)
5	Schønneman (p. 75)	12	Frama (p. 123)	19	Café Sommersko (p. 91)
6	Bottega Barlie (p. 71)	13	Tableau (p. 157)		
7	Bar Vitrine (p. 105)	14	Rue Verte (p. 137)		

The Inner City is the heart of Copenhagen, where tourists flock, drawn by the captivating charm of old-world Copenhagen and the new, fashionable lifestyle that has made the city one of the most talked-about destinations in the world. It offers an abundance of exciting places to explore, from key cultural attractions to exclusive shops, along with a wide variety of excellent food, drinks, and relaxing retreats.

You could easily spend several days exploring the city's art institutions, but don't miss the Glyptoteket (p. 176), with its ancient marble busts and lush, palm-filled Winter Garden. Another must-see museum is Charlottenborg Kunsthal (p. 168), one of Copenhagen's most beautiful contemporary art spaces, showcasing new artists and artwork since 1857.

Shopping in the Inner City could fill an entire weekend, but if your time is limited, focus on the areas around Ny Østergade, St. Regnegade, and Møntergade. Here, you'll find a curated selection of exclusive fashion and design shops, with the best of them featured in this book.

The Inner City is also home to many of the innovative restaurants that have cemented Copenhagen's status as one of the world's top food destinations.

KROGS

3
4
1
5
2
6

Refshaleøen

			More to Explore:
1	Copenhagen Contemporary (p. 173)	3	Reffen Street Food, Refshalevej 167, 1432 Copenhagen
2	La Banchina (p. 81)	4	Mikkeller Baghaven, Refshalevej 169B, 1432 Copenhagen
		5	Lille Bakery, Refshalevej 213B, 1432 Copenhagen
		6	Copenhill, Vindmøllevej 6, 2300 Copenhagen

Refshaleøen, once home to one of the world's largest shipyards in Copenhagen's harbor, has transformed into a thriving cultural and creative hub. Now a symbol of sustainability and innovation, it offers an eclectic mix of festivals, cutting-edge bars, restaurants, markets, and artist studios, all housed in repurposed industrial warehouses. Key attractions like Reffen Street food, Lille Bakery, and Café La Banchina (p. 80) perfectly capture the unique Refshaleøen vibe. For a one-of-a-kind experience, visitors can climb, hike, or ski year-round on CopenHill, a slope ingeniously designed by BIG Architects atop a waste-to-energy plant.

173 A

Refshaleøen

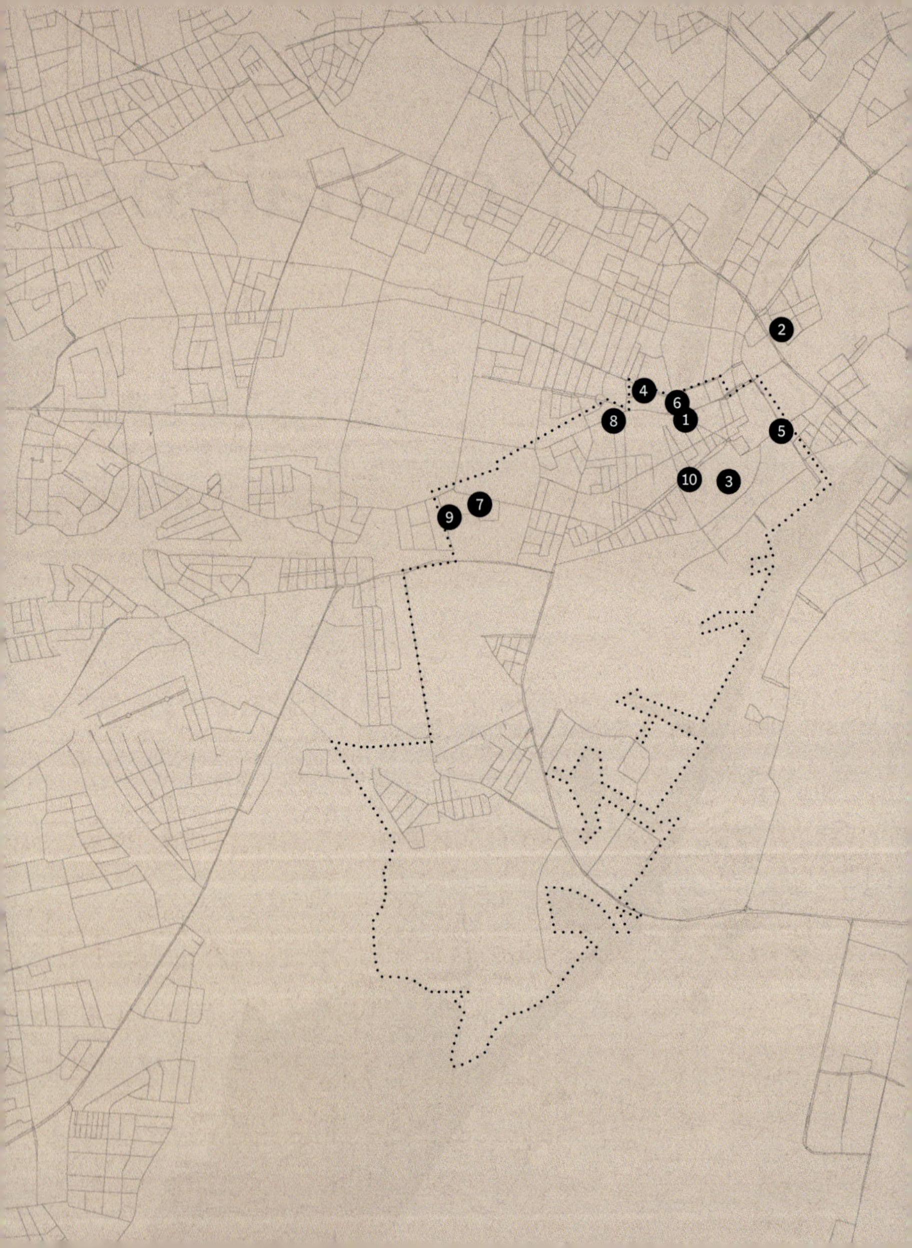

2
4
6
1
8
5
10
3
7
9

Vesterbro

1 Coco Hotel (p. 25)
2 Hotel Bella Grande (p. 33)
3 Åben (p. 85)
4 Central Hotel (p. 45)
5 Villa Copenhagen (p. 29)
6 Jerome Vintage (p. 149)
7 Hotel Ottilia (p. 39)

More to Explore:

8 Værnedamsvej, 1619 Copenhagen
9 Carlsbergbyen, Gamle Carlsberg Vej 10, 1799 Copenhagen
10 Prolog Coffee Bar, Høkerboderne 16, 1712 Copenhagen

Once a gritty neighborhood known for prostitution and drug addiction, Vesterbro has undergone a remarkable transformation since the 1990s. Today, it's a vibrant and dynamic district brimming with stylish hotels, trendy bars and restaurants in the Meatpacking District, and quirky second-hand shops along Istedgade and Vesterbrogade. The small shopping street Værnedamsvej is a must-see in Vesterbro. While it's often called "Little Paris," it feels more like a mix of everything. You can easily spend hours strolling back and forth along Værnedamsvej and Tullinsgade. On the outskirts of Vesterbro lies Carlsbergbyen, a brand-new district built on the site where the world-famous Carlsberg beer was once produced. New restaurants, bars, and shops are popping up, bringing urban life to the old brewery district. For a great dining and late-night experience, head to the Meatpacking District.

HART
19
21
HART
BREAD
COFFEE
PASTRIES
LUNCH

3
5
4
6
2
1

Nordhavn

1 Sandkaj Harbour Swiming (p. 195)

2 Andersen & Maillard (p. 49)

More to Explore:

3 Århusgade Quarter, 2150 Copenhagen

4 Atelier September, Århusgade 128D, 2150 Copenhagen

5 Konditaget Lüders, Helsinkigade 30, 2150 Copenhagen

6 Audo House, Århusgade 130, 2150 Copenhagen

Nordhavn (North Harbour) is Copenhagen's most successful urban development project, making it a must-see area. Originally a free port dominated by raw industry, Nordhavn has transformed into a green, vibrant neighbourhood brimming with life in the Århusgade quarter. In 2020, two metro stations, Sundkaj and Nordhavn, opened, further connecting the area to the rest of the city. Nordhavn boasts impressive new architecture, including Konditaget Lüders, a rooftop playground atop a multi-story parking garage that offers panoramic views of the sea. Urban development in Nordhavn is still ongoing, with many more buildings set to rise in the coming years. This transformation has drawn top architectural firms, including BIG (Bjarke Ingels Group) and Cobe Architects, both of which now have their headquarters in the area. Surrounded by water on all sides, Nordhavn also offers the chance to swim at the Sandkaj harbor bath. In addition to the metro, you can hop on the yellow harbor ferries, which provide quick routes to Refshaleøen, the Inner City, and Sydhavnen (South Harbour).

Audo
Audo

H·K·L·M·N
128 H

3
5
4
2
7
1
6

Christianshavn

			More to Explore:
1	Edition Copenhagen (p. 153)	6	Christiania, Bådsmandsstræde 43, 1407 Copenhagen
2	25hours Hotel Paper Island (p. 17)	7	Broens Street Food, Strandgade 95, 1401 Copenhagen
3	Kaj Hotel (p. 41)		
4	Operaparken (p. 185)		
5	Restaurant Væksthuset (p. 95)		

Christianshavn is technically an island nestled in the heart of Copenhagen, surrounded by water and connected to the rest of the city through its picturesque canals. Established in the 17th century as a bustling trading hub, it once served as a departure point for ships sailing from Christianshavn to destinations across the globe.

Today, Christianshavn is a charming and sought-after neighborhood, known for its stunning historic buildings lining the canals. The area boasts fantastic restaurants, small cafés, traditional "brown" pubs and intimate art galleries. Tucked away in the old courtyards, artist workshops and small craft businesses thrive, contributing to the vibrant lifestyle that hums around the waterways. Christianshavn is often associated with Christiania, the famous freetown established in the 1970s. Between Christianshavn and Refshaleøen lies Papirøen (Paper Island), once home to the beloved Copenhagen Street Food, now replaced by Broens Street Food, a smaller and more upscale version. The area is anchored by the iconic Opera House, designed by Henning Larsen Architects, and the newly established Opera Park (p. 184).

CHRISTIANSHAVN

3
6
7
8
5
1
2
4

Østerbro

			More to Explore:
1	Amator (p. 59)	5	Fælledparken, 2100 Copenhagen
2	Brasserie Post (p. 87)	6	Botega Estadio, Gunnar Nu Hansens Pl. 9, 2100 Copenhagen
3	Juno the Bakery (p. 55)	7	Østerbro Stadion, Gunnar Nu Hansens Pl. 7, 2100 Copenhagen
4	Studio Oliver Gustav (p. 145)	8	Nordre Frihavnsgade, 2100 Copenhagen

Østerbro is often recognized for its reputation as a relaxed and sophisticated neighborhood, largely residential and known for its quiet streets where strollers and joggers are a common sight. The area is dotted with small green spaces and larger parks, such as Fælledparken and Kastellet, which is open to the public and features a beautiful park where you can walk or jog along the ramparts.

But that's only part of the story. There's much more to Østerbro than meets the eye. Creative newcomers are injecting fresh energy into the area with innovative ideas and concepts. Nordre Frihavnsgade seamlessly blends traditional specialty shops with trendy eateries, wine bars, and coffee spots, creating a dynamic and evolving local scene. It's obvious that Østerbro also has a distinct sense of community. Even football has a stylish edge here. The local club B93 isn't supported by hooligans but by a fashionable young crowd sipping natural wine at Botega Estadio and enjoying vegan sausages during the game.

4
7
6
3
2
1
5

Nørrebro

More to Explore:

6 Jægerborgsgade, 2200 Copenhagen
7 Rentemestervej, 2400 Copenhagen

Every major city has its cultural melting pot, and in Copenhagen, that place is Nørrebro. Known for its vibrant creativity and multicultural atmosphere, this district is packed with small independent shops, cozy bars, cafés, and a wide array of outstanding restaurants. Streets like Jægersborggade, Rantzausgade, and Elmegade truly embody the unique character of Nørrebro. For a more peaceful retreat, you can visit the Assistens Cemetery (p. 166), where many locals relax in the sun during the summer. It is also the resting place of famous figures like H.C. Andersen and Søren Kierkegaard. Another popular gathering spot is Dronning Louises Bridge, which connects Nørrebro to the city center. To experience the more up-and-coming side of Nørrebro, head to Rentemestervej in the Nordvest district for a more edgy Berlin-inspired vibe.

1
2
3
4
5
6
7

Frederiksberg

			More to Explore:
1	Piola Pastificio (p. 93)	4	Frederiksberg Allé, 2000 Frederiksberg
2	Bar Amore (p. 99)	5	Sankt Thomas Plads, 2000 Frederiksberg
3	Bird (p. 109)	6	Gl. Kongevej, 2000 Frederiksberg
		7	Frederiksberg Have, 2000 Frederiksberg

Frederiksberg is a prestigious and upscale district in Copenhagen, known for its wealth, history, and independence. Technically its own municipality, but let's be real, it's an integral part of the city. Frederiksberg effortlessly combines laid-back luxury with diversity, offering tree-lined boulevards, exclusive shops, and cozy cafés that invite you to linger. It's easily accessible from the heart of Copenhagen, with Gammel Kongevej as its main artery, a lively shopping street packed with restaurants, fashion boutiques, and coffee spots.

Frederiksberg Allé is another standout, a grand boulevard with Parisian flair. Stroll along this elegant avenue and you'll pass the charming Sankt Thomas Plads before ending up at Frederiksberg Garden. This sprawling park is ideal for a lazy afternoon, whether you're taking in the lush scenery or catching a glimpse of the Copenhagen Zoo's famous elephant house.

ST-THOMAS

ANOTHER ASPECT

Another Aspect

Møntergade 3A
1116 Copenhagen

@another_aspect
anotheraspect.org
+45 4279 5397

Founded in 2019 by Daniel Brøndt, Anders Poulsen, and Nicolaj Thomsen, Another Aspect is built on the principles of sustainability and timeless design. Starting in a Vesterbro basement, they've since expanded into the heart of Copenhagen's fashion district with a 200 sqm flagship store on Møntergade. Designed by Studio 0405, the space combines brutalist architecture with warm, Danish oak cabinets and custom furniture. The aesthetic reflects their belief in mindful, long-lasting fashion as every material chosen for its durability and history.

The store isn't just for shopping, though. In partnership with La Cabra, they've built in one of Copenhagen's most hyped coffee bars, inviting everyone to linger, chat with the founders, and enjoy a slow moment amidst the curated pieces. It's a space designed for the community, where fashion meets culture in a laid-back yet thoughtfully designed environment.

Another Aspect, together with La Cabra, has created a fashion community around this location that is simply hard to beat.

ANOTHER ASPECT

Naked Copenhagen

Store Regnegade 2
1110 Copenhagen

@nakedcph
nakedcph.com
+45 3315 8380

Founded in 2004, Naked Copenhagen has emerged as the premier global destination for women's sneakers, distinctly challenging the male-dominated industry. Positioned at Store Regnegade 2 in the heart of Copenhagen, the flagship store is designed with women and community at its core. This space isn't just a retail location; it's also a lively spot where people come together to connect, inspire, and experience the essence of the Naked Copenhagen universe.

The store itself showcases Copenhagen's classic architectural elegance with a sculpted entrance, spanning 265 sqm to offer an extensive range of apparel, footwear, and lifestyle products. This flagship store marks a significant milestone in Naked Copenhagen's journey to redefine women's space in the sneaker industry.

Rue Verte

Ny Østergade 11
1101 Copenhagen

@rueverte
rueverte.dk
+45 3312 5555

Founded in 1994 by Michala Jessen, Rue Verte is a cornerstone of Copenhagen's vibrant design scene. Housed in a historic 1700s building, Rue Verte blends the charm of the past with contemporary sophistication, showcasing an exquisite mix of unique objects, vintage treasures, and art, alongside exclusive design objects and furniture. The studio's interior design consultants excel at crafting extraordinary, timeless spaces that reflect the individuality of each client. Rue Verte Gallery, located at the same address, displays works from both upcoming and established artists and designers that you won't find anywhere else in Denmark.

The setting embodies sleek Nordic minimalism, but inside, you'll uncover the finest Belgian, French, and Italian designs, unmatched anywhere else.

THE PARISIANS
AXEL VERVOORDT
PRIVATE SPACES
BESPOKE & BEYOND
A LIFE OF THINGS
Living with Wood
STILL
THINK
BELGIAN MODERN

New Mags

Ny Østergade 28
1101 Copenhagen

@new_mags
new-mags.com
+45 3139 0880

New Mags is more than a bookstore; it's a destination where art and literature converge, offering a select array of lifestyle books, magazines, and accessories. Founded in 2016 in Horsens, Jutland by Jesper Svangård and Jesper Oxholm Mikkelsen, the brand quickly outgrew its initial vision. Their dream of a space that not only stores but celebrates books culminated in the opening of their first showroom in Copenhagen in 2021.

Designed by Jonas Bjerre Poulsen of Norm Architects, the showroom exemplifies aesthetic refinement. Inspired by the grand libraries of the past century, it features a blend of natural materials that combine old-world charm with modern Nordic design. This environment does more than display books; it enhances their texture and color, inviting everyone to linger and explore. New Mags' showroom is a space that elevates lifestyle and design, making it a significant cultural spot for bibliophiles and design aficionados alike.

The space is much more than just a bookshop. It offers a highly aesthetic experience, featuring quality design and lifestyle books like this one.

LAYER

Studio Oliver Gustav

Kastelvej 18
2100 Copenhagen

@studiooliverg ustav
olivergustav.com
+45 2737 4630

Studio Oliver Gustav, envisioned by Copenhagen-based designer Oliver Gustav, transforms a historic museum building into a sanctuary of design and artistry. Beyond its unassuming facade lies a realm of timeless simplicity and quiet grandeur, reflecting Oliver's unique aesthetic of melancholic purity. The studio features his own line of furniture and limited-edition objects, alongside carefully curated international designs, rare antiques, and exquisite curiosities that embody sustainability and craftsmanship.

Each item, selected with deep personal commitment, aims to transport visitors to distant lands through their story and design. With over 15 years of global exploration, Oliver has crafted a design style that defies conventional labels, offering a hypnotic, monochromatic experience that engages the senses. At Studio Oliver Gustav, you're not just visiting a space; you're embarking on a multisensory journey of art, travel, and introspective discovery.

Studio Oliver Gustav is a masterclass in excellence. Stepping into this enchanting space takes you on a multisensory journey through art, travel, and introspective discovery.

Jerome Vintage

Vesterbrogade 36
1620 Copenhagen

@jerome_vintage
wearephoenix.dk
+45 4013 6804

In the pulsing heart of Vesterbro, Jerome and Rosy Vintage stand as a sanctuary for vintage lovers and fashion enthusiasts. Founded with passion by Pia Kierulff and Mai-Britt Gamdrup Jonsen in 2014 and 2019 respectively, these sister stores have become Copenhagen's go-to destinations for vintage collectors and style savants. Jerome Vintage, the elder of the two, initially set out to inspire a lifestyle steeped in high-end vintage fashion, featuring everything from Metallica tees to elegant YSL blazers. Rosy Vintage complements this with a diverse array of non-branded vintage finds, making elite fashion accessible to all.

The stores exude a calm elegance, with sleek, minimalist decor that allows the meticulously curated collections to shine, from iconic labels like Christian Dior and Hermès to Jerome Studio's bespoke wedding gowns and luxurious pyjamas.

Jerome Vintage is far from your typical vintage store. With its chic concept and carefully curated high-end pieces, this spot is an absolute must-visit.

Edition Copenhagen

Strandgade 66
1401 Copenhagen

@editioncopenhagen
editioncopenhagen.com
+45 3254 3311

Founded in 1959, Edition Copenhagen stands as one of the world's foremost lithographic workshops. Located in the heart of Christianshavn in Copenhagen, the spacious workshop and gallery are housed in a distinctive industrial building. Visitors can explore and purchase from a vast collection of artworks created in collaboration with both emerging and established artists. However, the true magic happens within the workshop itself, where all of Edition Copenhagen's original lithographs are crafted. The printing process in the workshop is performed according to traditional techniques dating back to the 18th century. Only one artist works in the workshop at a time and is supported by three expert lithographers with the finest technical skills.

Nuvole Design

St. Regnegade 2
1101 Copenhagen

@nuvole.design
nuvole.design
+45 2974 9429

Nuvole, founded in 2020 by sisters Marlene Bernth and Louise Bernth Olsen, redefines the concept of retail. With a background in innovative projects such as Holly Golightly and Collage The Shop, the duo has crafted a unique space that transcends the traditional shopping experience.

At Nuvole, the focus isn't on endless inventory. Instead, it serves as a curated platform where fashion and interior brands book space for a week or more to showcase their creations. This ever-changing selection provides shoppers with access to rare finds and exclusive collections. Brands like Maison Hotel, Palorosa, and Swedish Dusty Deco make regular appearances, offering a blend of impeccable style and craftsmanship. Beyond its distinctive product offerings, Nuvole also delivers expert advice on interior design and personalised shopping, transforming it into more than just a concept store.

TABLEAU

Tableau

St. Strandstræde 20
1255 Copenhagen

@tableau_cph
tableau-cph.com
+45 3145 3130

Tableau is a multidisciplinary creative studio, exhibition space, and shop located in a historic heritage building on the iconic Store Strandstræde, just a stone's throw from the lively Kongens Nytorv and Nyhavn. Built in 1789, the well-preserved original interior of this 18th century merchant's shop offers a striking contrast to Tableau's industrial aesthetic, enhanced by an abundance of fresh flowers. Moving forward, the new store will serve as a wunderkammer of small objects created by Tableau's community of artists and designers, alongside fresh bouquets and floral installations.

In addition to the exhibition space and concept store, the Tableau studio, founded in 2018, specializes in floral design, object design, exhibition design, interior design, and architectural installations. Their past projects include collaborations with prestigious brands such as Hermès, Tom Dixon, and Vogue, among others.

This store is a magical *Wunderkammer* filled with small art and design objects, and beautifully paired with artistically styled bouquets of fresh flowers.

Thorvaldsens Museum
Assistens Cemetery
Kunsthal Charlottenborg
Copenhagen Contemporary
Ny Carlsberg Glyptotek
Designmuseum Danmark
Operaparken
Louisiana Museum of Modern Art
The Royal Library Gardens
Harbour Swimming

Explore

Thorvaldsens Museum

Bertel Thorvaldsens Plads 2
1312 Copenhagen

@thorvaldsensmuseum
thorvaldsensmuseum.dk
+45 2168 7568

Bold colors and striking architectural design define this iconic museum in the heart of Copenhagen, home to the works of renowned Danish sculptor Bertel Thorvaldsen (1770–1844). Not only does it showcase his magnificent sculptures, but it also houses his personal collection of paintings and antiquities. A walk through the museum is a mesmerizing experience of brightly coloured walls, richly decorated ceilings, mosaic floors, and natural inflow of light. At the heart of it all are Thorvaldsen's stunning marble and plaster sculptures, commanding attention in every room. Since its opening in 1848 as Denmark's first museum, Thorvaldsen's Museum has provided visitors with a unique opportunity to immerse themselves in world-class art, surrounded by breathtaking architectural beauty.

Even if plaster sculptures and ancient marble busts aren't your thing, the museum's vibrant colours are reason enough to pay it a visit.

Assistens Cemetery

Kapelvej 2
2200 Copenhagen

kk.dk
+45 3366 9100

Tucked away in the vibrant neighborhood of Nørrebro, Assistens Cemetery is more than just a final resting place, it's a peaceful haven where life and reflection intertwine. Established in 1760, this historic churchyard remains active today. When it first opened, sailors brought exotic plants from distant lands, including South America, India, and Japan, which now grace the cemetery with a colorful display of blooms and foliage.

Today, Assistens Cemetery not only serves as a burial ground but also as a spot where locals come to bask in the sun, celebrate birthdays, or enjoy a quiet picnic. Hence, the cemetery's atmosphere is unlike any other, offering a rare combination of serenity and community spirit.

Some of the most iconic figures are buried here, including the philosopher Søren Kierkegaard and writer Hans Christian Andersen, alongside a host of the nation's celebrated writers, musicians, and cultural figures.

CHARLOTTENBORG
KUNSTUDSTILLING

Kunsthal Charlottenborg

Nyhavn 2
1051 Copenhagen

@kunsthalcharlottenborg
kunsthalcharlottenborg.dk
+45 3374 4639

Kunsthal Charlottenborg stands as one of Northern Europe's premier contemporary art venues. Since 1883, it has played a pivotal role in the art scene, offering an ever-evolving exhibition program that highlights both emerging talents and established artists from around the globe. True to its name, Kunsthal Charlottenborg does not feature permanent exhibitions. Instead, it hosts a dynamic rotation of shows, complemented by a lively schedule of artist talks, performances, concerts, and film screenings. The venue also houses the renowned Motto Bookstore, offering a curated selection of art books, magazines, and literature on design and theory. In the courtyard, you'll find Apollo Bar, a once modest café that Danish chef Frederik Bille Brahe has transformed into a cultural hotspot for Copenhagen's creative crowd in fashion, design, and art.

If you're lucky or time your visit just right, don't miss the chance to experience Charlottenborg's regular Spring and Autumn exhibitions.

Copenhagen Contemporary

Refshalevej 173A
1432 Copenhagen

@copenhagen_contemporary
copenhagencontemporary.org
+45 2989 8087

Copenhagen Contemporary is a must-visit destination for anyone interested in cutting-edge art. Located in the expansive, repurposed B&W welding hall on Refshaleøen, this international art center offers 7,000 sqm of raw, industrial space, perfectly suited to the ambitious scale of the installations, performances, and video works it showcases.

Since its founding in 2016, Copenhagen Contemporary has hosted exhibitions by some of the biggest names in contemporary art, including Yoko Ono, Bruce Nauman, and Claudia Comte. From Copenhagen Contemporary, you can step out into Refshaleøen, grab a bite from the Copenhagen Street Food market, or simply enjoy the view of Copenhagen's harbour.

The combination of Copenhagen Contemporary and a visit to Refshaleøen is a must-see for anyone seeking cutting-edge experiences.

Ny Carlsberg Glyptotek

Dantes Plads 7
1556 Copenhagen

@glyptoteket
glyptoteket.dk
+45 3341 8141

At Ny Carlsberg Glyptotek, you will encounter a unique combination of outstanding art and architecture. Located in the center of Copenhagen, the monumental building, dating back to 1897, is a work of art in itself. Step inside, and you're transported through time. From the ancient wonders of Egypt, Rome, and Greece to the refined beauty of French impressionism and the Danish Golden Age, the collection is a rich tapestry of global art history. Sculptures by Rodin and paintings by Gauguin and Monet stand proudly next to works from Denmark's most celebrated artists. Retreat to the beautiful winter garden, where palm trees and lush greenery surround a tranquil fountain. It's the perfect spot to enjoy coffee or a light lunch.

The Glyptotek is a true oasis in the heart of the city, where art and architecture blend in extraordinary harmony. It's a place everyone should experience.

CARL · OTTILIA IACOBSEN

Designmuseum Danmark

Bredgade 68
1260 Copenhagen

@designmuseumdanmark
designmuseum.dk
+45 3318 5656

Step into the heart of Danish design heritage at Designmuseum Danmark, located in Copenhagen's historic district. Here, you'll encounter the proud tradition of Danish and international design, showcased through the museum's extensive collection of iconic pieces and visionary exhibitions that explore the future of design. From Victorian homes and past collection obsessions to today's innovative trends, the museum's exhibitions address both timeless aesthetics and global issues.

Since 1926, Designmuseum Danmark has been housed in one of Copenhagen's finest rococo buildings, the former Royal Frederik's Hospital. In the 1920s, architects Ivar Bentsen and Kaare Klint renovated and adapted the space for museum use, with Klint himself designing the museum's furnishings. The museum garden is open to the public daily and free of charge. It's a tranquil setting for exhibitions and events, with a museum café offering outdoor seating nestled among the greenery.

Danish design is celebrated worldwide. This is the perfect place to immerse yourself in its history and uncover the full story behind its iconic status.

Operaparken

Ekvipagemestervej 18
1438 Copenhagen

operaparkfonden.dk

The Opera Park is the city's newest recreational area and stands in stark contrast to the many modern glass buildings that otherwise dominate the waterfront. For more than 20 years, this humble green spot next to the Opera House remained completely untouched. Fortunately, the site has been allowed to stay green. However, beneath the green surface, a parking garage with space for 300 cars has been constructed to benefit the Opera's guests. The Opera scene has inspired the park's layout, which is structured as foreground, middle ground, and background, where trees and plants are strategically placed so that their heights create a landscape that opens up toward the harbour. In the park's pavilion, you'll find the greenhouse, which houses a restaurant and café open year-round, even in winter. The Opera Park is a donation from the A. P. Møller Foundation as a recreational area in Copenhagen. The park is designed by Cobe Architects and is centrally located between the modern Paper Island and the historic Holmen, with its well-preserved buildings.

Operaparken offers a stunning landscape architecture experience on the newly established Paper Island. While you're there, take a tour around Holmen.

Louisiana Museum of Modern Art

Gl Strandvej 13
3050 Humlebæk

@louisianamuseum
louisiana.dk
+45 4919 0719

The Louisiana Museum of Modern Art is one of the most beloved art destinations in the world, known not just for its impressive collection, but also for how beautifully it blends with its surroundings. Located 30 minutes north of Copenhagen, in the coastal village of Humlebæk, the museum sits along the Øresund Strait, offering peaceful views of southern Sweden and a beautiful sculpture park where art meets nature.

What sets Louisiana apart is its thoughtful architecture. When founder Knud W. Jensen brought in architects Jørgen Bo and Wilhelm Wohlert, they aimed to merge the museum with its seaside setting. The result is a series of modernist pavilions that connect naturally with the landscape, seamlessly blending indoor and outdoor spaces. It's a place where art and nature feel intertwined, leaving visitors with an experience that lingers long after their visit.

What more can be said about Louisiana that hasn't already been said or written? Probably the best art museum in the world.

The Royal Library Gardens

Proviantpassagen 1
1218 Copenhagen

slks.dk
+45 3395 4200

The Royal Library Garden is a hidden gem in the heart of Copenhagen, tucked away between Christiansborg Palace and the Royal Library. Few people in the city know about this peaceful retreat, making it far less crowded than some of Copenhagen's more popular parks.

Designed in 1920 by Jens Peder Andersen and Thorvald Jørgensen, the garden was built on the grounds of what was once Christian IV's naval port. At its center stands a bronze statue of Danish philosopher Søren Kierkegaard, sculpted by Louis Hasselriis in 1918, adding a touch of quiet contemplation to the serene atmosphere.

Whether you're looking to catch some sun or enjoy a takeaway coffee, the Royal Library Garden is the perfect spot to unwind between exploring Copenhagen's bustling shopping streets.

Poliform

Harbour Swimming

Like many major city harbours, Copenhagen's was once polluted with sewage, industrial waste, and oil spills. However, thanks to an ambitious cleanup project in the 1990s, it has undergone a remarkable transformation, now ranking as a top destination for year-round swimming. Today, locals enjoy dipping into various harbour swimming spots, and for those seeking a winter challenge, the Sandkaj Harbor Bath in the Nordhavn district stays open all year.

In 2002, Copenhagen introduced its first havnebad (harbour bath) at Islands Brygge, just a short distance from the Inner city. This facility offers five pools and three diving boards, making it a favourite spot for locals and visitors alike. Other popular spots include the Sandkaj Harbor Bath, a year-round facility in a former industrial port. Since 2015, membership in the city's winter bathing clubs has doubled, and last year, Copenhagen added its first public saunas, further enriching the city's vibrant swimming culture.

Copenhagen's success with harbour swimming has inspired other major cities, like London and Paris, to invest in cleaning their waterways and creating public swimming facilities for their residents.

Index

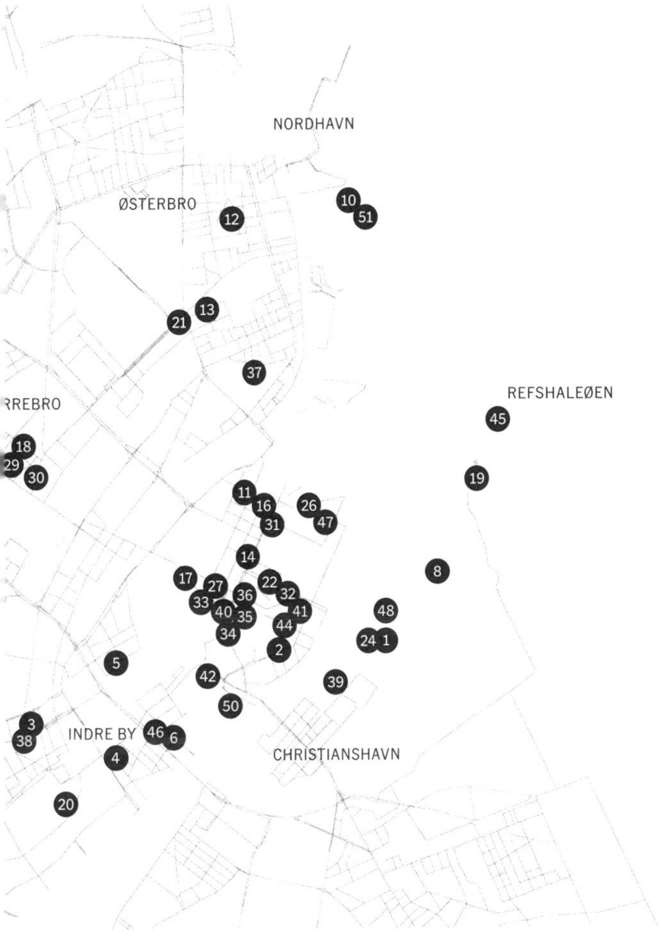

NORDHAVN

ØSTERBRO

REFSHALEØEN

RREBRO

INDRE BY

CHRISTIANSHAVN

Scan to get the map

28 Bird (p. 109)
29 Pompette (p. 113)
30 Trine Tuxen Jewelry (p. 119)
31 Frama (p. 123)
32 Helle Mardahl Studio (p. 127)
33 Another Aspect (p. 131)
34 Naked Copenhagen (p. 135)
35 Rue Verte (p. 137)
36 New Mags (p. 141)
37 Studio Oliver Gustav (p. 145)
38 Jerome Vintage (p. 149)
39 Edition Copenhagen (p. 153)
40 Nuvole Design (p. 155)
41 Tableau (p. 157)
42 Thorvaldsens Museum (p. 163)
43 Assistens Cemetery (p. 167)
44 Kunsthal Charlottenborg (p. 169)
45 Copenhagen Contemporary (p. 173)
46 Ny Carlsberg Glyptotek (p. 177)
47 Designmuseum Danmark (p. 181)
48 Operaparken (p. 185)
49 Louisiana Museum (p. 189)
50 The Royal Library Gardens (p. 193)
51 Harbour Swimming (p. 195)

ABOUT THE EDITOR

Mads Arlien-Søborg is a Copenhagen-based journalist and lifestyle expert. He holds a master's degree in modern Culture and Communication from University of Copenhagen. Mads has worked with design, fashion and lifestyles for many years. He has hosted several television shows about travel, design and architecture.

New Mags is more than a bookstore; it's a destination where art and literature converge, offering a select array of lifestyle books, magazines, and accessories. Founded in 2016 in Horsens, Jutland by Jesper Svangård and Jesper Oxholm Mikkelsen. Their dream of a space that not only stores but celebrates books culminated in the opening of their first showroom in Copenhagen in 2021.

NOTES

NOTES

PHOTO CREDITS

FRONT COVER & DESTINATION
© Tobias Glud

NEIGHBOURHOODS
© Mads Arlien-Søborg

STAY
25hours Papirøen © Stephan Lemke
Central Hotel: © Jon Norstrøm
Coco Hotel: Courtesy of Coco Hotel
Hotel Bella Grande: Courtesy of Bella Grande
Hotel Ottilia: © Rozbeh Zavari, Sasha Maslov
Hotel Sanders: Courtesy of Hotel Sanders
Kaj Hotel: Courtesy of Kaj Hotel
Nobis Copenhagen: © Søren Kristensen
Villa Copenhagen: Courtesy of Villa Copenhagen

TASTE
Åben: © Paula Hincenberga
Amator: © Paolo Galgani
Andersen & Maillard: © Danielle Siggerud
Atelier September: Courtesy of Atelier September
Bar Amore: © Magnus Omme
Bar Vitrine: © Nefeli Have for Frama
Bird: © Goran Aziz
Bottega Barlie: © Frederikke Svarre
Brasserie Post: Courtesy of Brasserie Post
Flere Fugle: © Ejvind Spence
Graziano: © Kasper Kristoffersen
Juno Bakery: © Michael Gardenia
La Banchina: © Anders Hviid, Esther Karczag
Lille Blå: Courtesy of Lille Blå
Piola Pastificio: Courtesy of Piola Pastificio
Pompette: © Olivia Rohde
Schønnemann: Courtesy of Schønnemann
Studio x Kitchen: © Maya Matsuura, Gabija Seredaite, Marlene Ann Lough, Mayuko Takyu
Væksthuset: Courtesy of Væksthuset
Cafe Sommersko: © Flemming Gernyx

SHOP
Another Aspect: Courtesy of Another Aspect
Frama: Courtesy of Frama
Jerome Vintage: Courtesy of Jerome Vintage
Naked Copenhagen: Courtesy of Naked Copenhagen
New Mags: © Jonas Bjerre Poulsen, Sandie Lykke
Oliver Gustav: Courtesy of Oliver Gustav
Rue Verte: Courtesy of Rue Verte
Saks Potts: © Frederik Kastrupsen
Tableau: © Andre Papini
Trine Tuxen: © Claus Troelsgaard
Helle Mardahl: © Alastair Philip Wiper
Edition Copenhagen: © Mellanie Gandø

EXPLORE
Assistens Cemetery: © Wonderful Copenhagen
Kunsthal Charlottenborg: © David Stjernholm, Lars Engelgaar, Joakim Züger
Copenhagen Contemporary: © Adam Mørk, David Stjernholm, Farzad Soleimani, Anders Sune Berg
The Royal Library Gardens: © Thomas Rahbek
Ny Carlsberg Glyptotek: © Ana Cecilia Gonzalez
Louisiana Museum of Modern Art: © Kim Hansen
Operaparken: © Henriette Lunn, Copenhagen drone
Thorvaldsens Museum: © Sarah Coghill
Harbour Swimming: © Visit Copenhagen
Designmuseum Denmark: © Designmuseum Denmark, Rasmus Hjortshøj, Christian Hoyer, Luka Hesselberg

NEW MAGS CITY GUIDE
COPENHAGEN

Editor-In-Chief: Mads Arlien-Søborg
Publisher: New Mags
Sales: Jesper Svangård, New Mags

Art Direction: Studio8585
Design Director: Mario Depicolzuane
Design & Layout: Benja Pavlin, Varshini KVSS

ISBN: 978-87-94190-72-5

1st Edition 2025
Printed at GPS Group, 2025

Published in 2025 by New Mags.

New Mags, Office & Distribution
Vejlevej 13, 8700 Horsens, Denmark
new-mags.com

NEW MAGS

This book contains a curated selection of the editor's favourite places and should be used for its intended purpose, as a guide. It is by no means comprehensive of all the amazing locations the city has to offer. Since changes may have occurred since publication, we recommend using the contact information for each location to ensure up-to-date details.

The editor and publisher wish to express their gratitude to everyone who played a role in making this book possible: the staff, friends and families, brands, and organizations. A big thank you to Fujifilm® for giving us the opportunity to create beautiful city images for the book.